CAREERS FOR HEROES

BOMB SQUADS

Lee Fitzgerald

PowerKiDS press

New York

Published in 2016 by The Rosen Publishing Group, Inc.
29 East 21st Street, New York, NY 10010

First Edition

Editor: Katie Kawa
Book Design: Mickey Harmon

Photo Credits: Cover (man in foreground) cbarnesphotography/E+/Getty Images; cover (background), p. 7 Dumitrescu Ciprian-Florin/Shutterstock.com; cover, pp. 1, 3, 4, 6, 8, 10, 12, 14, 16, 18–19, 20, 22–24 (gray and yellow textures) siro46/Shutterstock.com; p. 5 Photoprofi30/Shutterstock.com; p. 6 LukaTDB/Shutterstock.com; p. 9 https://www.flickr.com/photos/ekavet/3686245363/in/photolist-6BJYjz-6sRNxj-6BJYjt-6sRNxh-6sMCRv-6BJYja-6BJYjx-6sMCRD-6sMCRB-aepau4-6sMCRg-6sMCR6-6sMCRK-6BJYjg-4Mg3sT-6swTzt-eb2Dy8-6sB1Ku;
p. 11 Don Bendickson/Shutterstock.com; p. 13 MANDEL NGAN/Staff/AFP/Getty Images; p. 15 https://commons.wikimedia.org/wiki/File:US_Navy_030605-N-5862D-011_Aviation_Ordnanceman_1st_Class_Jeff_Kuhar,_wearing_a_bomb_suit,_uses_a_manipulator_to_pick_up_a_simulated_suspect_explosive_aboard_Naval_Submarine_Base_King%27s_Bay,_Ga.jpg; p. 17 https://commons.wikimedia.org/wiki/File:Afghan_National_Army_Counter_IED_Specialist_at_Work_in_Afghanistan_MOD_45153490.jpg; p. 20 https://en.wikipedia.org/wiki/United_States_Capitol_Police#/media/File:Patch_of_the_United_States_Capitol_Police.png; p. 21 SAUL LOEB/Staff/AFP/Getty Images; p. 22 https://commons.wikimedia.org/wiki/File:An_Iraqi_explosive_ordnance_disposal_(EOD)_soldier_demonstrates_the_mobility_of_an_EOD_bomb_disposal_suit_during_EOD_training_in_the_Kirkuk_province_of_Iraq_Aug._28,_2010_100828-A-DM673-312.jpg.

Cataloging-in-Publication Data

Fitzgerald, Lee.
Bomb squads / by Lee Fitzgerald.
p. cm. — (Careers for heroes)
Includes index.
ISBN 978-1-5081-4394-9 (pbk.)
ISBN 978-1-5081-4395-6 (6-pack)
ISBN 978-1-5081-4396-3 (library binding)
1. Bomb squads — Juvenile literature. I. Fitzgerald, Lee. II. Title.
HV8080.B65 F58 2016
363.17'98—d23

Manufactured in the United States of America

CPSIA Compliance Information: Batch #BW16PK: For Further Information contact Rosen Publishing, New York, New York at 1-800-237-9932

CONTENTS

A DANGEROUS JOB

A bomb is a device made to explode under certain conditions. Bombs can be used to harm people and destroy property. Luckily, bomb squads around the United States work hard every day to **protect** us from these dangerous, or unsafe, explosive **devices**.

Members of bomb squads investigate, or closely study, packages and devices that could contain bombs. If they find a bomb, it's their job to keep it from harming anyone. They use the latest **technology** to keep themselves and the public as safe as possible. Does this sound like an exciting career? Read on to learn more about being part of a bomb squad!

FAST FACT!

Bomb squads exist on city, county, state, and national levels. The Federal Bureau of Investigation (FBI) has a national bomb squad unit, or team, made up of men and women called special agent bomb technicians (SABTs).

As technology advanced, bomb squads began using robots to check for explosives. Robots help keep members of bomb squads out of harm's way whenever possible, but this career is still very dangerous.

BOMB SQUAD BASICS

Bomb squads are generally smaller units within larger police departments or other **law enforcement agencies**, such as the FBI. The men and women who work as part of a bomb squad have to pass many tests along the way to make sure they can handle this line of work.

Bomb squads respond to calls of **suspicious** items that could be explosives. These could include illegal fireworks, **improvised explosive devices** (IEDs), or military weapons, which are called ordnance. Bomb squad members are trained to handle all kinds of explosives—even very dangerous bombs that could spread deadly **chemicals** or sicknesses.

FAST FACT!

Not all members of bomb squads are people! Many bomb squads use police dogs that are trained to detect, or find, explosives using their strong sense of smell.

If you want to be a member of a bomb squad, you need to be able to work as part of a team. Members of these teams are often called bomb technicians.

STARTING IN NEW YORK

Bomb squads have been working to protect people in the United States for over 110 years. In 1903, the New York Police Department (NYPD) Bomb Squad was formed to fight groups who used explosives to scare wealthy Italians and get money from them. For this reason, it was first known as the Italian Squad.

The NYPD Bomb Squad continued to grow and change over the years. It's the largest and oldest bomb squad of any U.S. city. However, the exact number of men and women who are a part of this squad isn't made known to the public.

FAST FACT!

It's not easy to join the NYPD Bomb Squad. Some years, the NYPD only accepts 10 percent of the people—or 1 out of every 10—who apply for a job with this squad.

The NYPD Bomb Squad has a long history of protecting the people of New York City.

ROBOTIC HELPERS

Things have come a long way since the early days of the NYPD Bomb Squad. Today, bomb squads around the United States are using technology that sometimes looks like it came out of a science-fiction movie!

Robots are a valuable part of bomb squads. They can do most of the tasks human bomb technicians do without endangering human lives. Robots have cameras that send streaming video to bomb technicians. They also have claws that act as hands to open car doors. Robots can even carry tools to break a bomb apart without a person ever touching the bomb.

FAST FACT!

Robots used by bomb squads often have X-ray **equipment**. X-rays are used to check suspicious packages for bombs.

Do you like building machines? If you do, you might be interested in a career creating the robots used by bomb squads. You'll need to study science and math to follow this career path.

OUT OF HARM'S WAY

While robots do a lot of work for bomb squads by people still play a very important part in this line of work. Bomb squad members must stay calm and help others stay calm in scary **situations**. The ability to think clearly in a dangerous situation is an important skill all bomb squad members must have.

Bomb squad members are often responsible for leading the evacuation of an area if they think a suspicious package or car contains a bomb. An evacuation is when people are removed from a dangerous place.

FAST FACT!

Bomb squad members are taught to treat each suspicious package or car as if it contains a bomb until proven otherwise.

If a bomb does go off, bomb squads work to make sure no one is around to be hurt by it. This is why they clear areas and shut down streets that could be too close to a possible explosion.

DESTROYING THE DEVICE

After a bomb squad clears the area around a suspicious package, a robot often goes to work by taking videos and X-rays of the device. If the bomb technicians believe it's an explosive device, they often use the robot to **disrupt** or destroy it.

In most cases, bomb squads don't want the entire device destroyed, because they want to study it later. However, there are some cases in which a robot takes the device to an empty, safe area. Then, the device is blown up to destroy it. This is called a controlled detonation. Bomb squad members oversee this from a safe place away from the explosion.

FAST FACT!

Bomb squads sometimes take pieces of a bomb to a forensics lab to be studied after it's no longer considered dangerous. A forensics lab is a place where pieces of evidence—things left behind at a crime scene—are studied.

Bomb squad members need to study the technology used in their robots in order to control them. They also need to study the science and technology behind explosive devices so they know what kinds of dangers they're dealing with every day.

SUITS FOR SAFETY

Even if a bomb squad uses robots, the people who make up the squad need to be prepared to go into a dangerous situation. Sometimes the robot falls over or doesn't work properly, and it's up to people to handle the bomb.

For this reason, bomb squad members also have access to X-rays and tools to render bombs safe, or make them unable to explode and hurt people. They also wear heavy suits meant to keep them safe in an explosion. These suits have a large helmet to protect their head. Blast plates in the suit are meant to protect them from flying pieces of metal called shrapnel.

FAST FACT!

The suits worn by bomb squad members are made to protect their back, too. This is because a big explosion could easily push a person backward, causing them to land hard on their back.

It's always dangerous working with bombs. However, bomb squad members have the most advanced gear to help them stay as safe as possible in case there's an explosion.

SCHOOL FOR BOMB SQUADS

If you want to become a member of a bomb squad, you need to be prepared to go through some tough training. Members of bomb squads around the United States train at the FBI Hazardous Devices School (HDS), which is located at the U.S. Army's Redstone Arsenal in Huntsville, Alabama. This is the only school in the country that offers national **certification** for bomb technicians.

Each police department or law enforcement agency runs its own continuing training exercises for its bomb squad members. They often train at least once a week to keep their skills sharp.

FAST FACT!

Bomb squad members who work with police dogs go through separate training to be the dog's handler. The dog then goes to live with its handler, and their training continues throughout the dog's career.

Subjects Taught at the HDS

1	chemistry (the science of matter and the changes it can go through)
2	physics (the science of matter and energy)
3	robot control
4	defusing a bomb (preventing it from exploding) by hand
5	recognizing and defusing bombs in different situations
6	safety
7	working while wearing a bomb suit

These are some of the many things bomb squad members learn during their six weeks at the HDS. Every three years, they must be re-certified through this school.

A SCARE IN WASHINGTON

Members of bomb squads hope they never have to use the training they go through in Huntsville. However, when they're faced with a dangerous situation, that training can help save lives.

In May 2015, members of the Capitol Police Hazardous Devices Section in Washington, D.C., sprang into action when a suspicious car was found near the U.S. Capitol with a pressure cooker inside it. Pressure cookers have been used to make bombs in the past. This bomb squad then used a controlled detonation to destroy the pressure cooker and other items. Nothing dangerous was ultimately found in the car.

FAST FACT!

Police officers often warn the public when a bomb squad will be detonating a possible bomb in a controlled setting. This helps avoid a sense of panic when people hear the loud explosions.

Members of bomb squads, such as the Capitol Police Hazardous Devices Section, must always be ready to go into a dangerous situation. Their training has prepared them to save many lives, including their own.

ANYTHING BUT BORING

Bomb squads are called in to investigate some very scary situations. They never know if the package they're investigating is harmless or if it contains a deadly explosive device. Because of this, they need to always be alert and ready to rely on their training to keep people safe.

A career as a member of a bomb squad is anything but boring. It's filled with danger, but it's also filled with opportunities to help people and even save lives. If you study and train hard enough, you could become a brave member of a bomb squad someday!

GLOSSARY

certification: Official approval to do something for a living.

chemical: Matter that can be mixed with other matter to cause changes.

device: A tool used for a certain purpose.

disrupt: To break apart in a way that causes something to be unable to continue in its usual way.

equipment: The tools needed for a certain purpose.

improvised explosive device: A bomb made and used in ways other than standard military explosives.

law enforcement agency: A government department that is formed with the purpose of making sure laws are followed.

protect: To keep safe.

situation: All the facts, conditions, and events that affect someone or something in a certain time and place.

suspicious: Causing a feeling that something is wrong.

technology: The use of science to invent useful things or to solve problems. Also, the tools or methods created this way.

INDEX

WEBSITES

Due to the changing nature of Internet links, PowerKids Press has developed an online list of websites related to the subject of this book. This site is updated regularly. Please use this link to access the list: www.powerkidslinks.com/chero/bmbsq